T0197444

Baseball with D

Danielle N Calhoun

AuthorHouse™
1663 Liberty Drive
Bloomington, IN 47403
www.authorhouse.com
Phone: 1 (800) 839-8640

Published by AuthorHouse 01/10/2019

ISBN: 978-1-5462-1112-9 (sc)
ISBN: 978-1-5462-1111-2 (e)

Library of Congress Control Number: 2018914237

Print information available on the last page.

Any people depicted in stock imagery provided by Getty Images are models,
and such images are being used for illustrative purposes only.
Certain stock imagery © Getty Images.

This book is printed on acid-free paper.

authorHOUSE®

Baseball with D

Hi everyone, my name is D.

Do you want to come play baseball with me?

You'll need some cleats,

You'll need a hat,

You'll need a glove,

And a baseball bat.

Now, we have bases...

One, two and three

The ultimate goal is to get home free.

So, make sure you run and don't get any outs.

You'll have to make it home,

That's what the game is all about!

Now when it's your time to bat,

Be sure to hit it out the park.

Even if you don't,

Just run to your mark.

First place,

Second place,

Third place,

Home!

Now that we've won the game

We can get ice cream and go home.

What color hat did D have on?

How many friends did D play baseball with?

Name two things D and his friends needed in order to play baseball?

What did D and his friend eat at the end of the game?

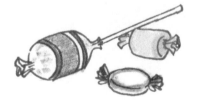